GIFTS FROM NATURE

Potpourri and Scented Gifts

GIFTS FROM NATURE

POTPOURRI AND SCENTED GIFTS

Creating natural fragrances for the home

JOANNE RIPPIN

LORENZ BOOKS
LONDON • NEW YORK • SYDNEY • BATH

This edition published in 1997 by Lorenz Books

Lorenz Books is an imprint of
Anness Publishing Limited
Hermes House
88-89 Blackfriars Road
London SE1 8HA

© 1997 Anness Publishing Limited

ISBN 1 85967 499 2

A CIP catalogue record for this book is available from the British Library

Publisher: Joanna Lorenz
Project Editor: Joanne Rippin
Editor: Beverley Jollands
Illustrator: Anna Koska
Designers: Lisa Tai and Lilian Lindblom

Printed and bound in Singapore

1 3 5 7 9 10 8 6 4 2

CONTENTS

INTRODUCTION

*B*efore the days of proper sanitation and hot running water the odours of day-to-day life were, at times, almost overpowering, and scents, unguents and perfumes were essential to lighten the atmosphere. Dried herbs were burnt in fireplaces and floors were strewn with the stems of fragrant lavender, rosemary and sage. Bowls were filled with dried scented roses to sweeten the air and different blends, using a range of perfumed flowers, were used to create a floral scent for each room. Centuries later, such mixtures are now more popular than ever, appreciated as much for the therapeutic pleasure of making them as for the subtle combinations of colours, textures and aromas they offer.

Potpourri recipes are infinitely variable and you can compose mixtures biased towards sweet, citrus or pungent accents to suit your personal preference. Whether you are making potpourri as a gift or to scent your own home, let the season influence your choice of materials: put together warm, spicy mixtures at Christmas; fresh, delicate woodland ones in spring. Make your summer mixtures a distillation of the floral abundance in your garden.

Scented sachets, bags and little cushions offer a host of possibilities for using potpourri. Ideal for lending their gentle fragrance to cupboards and drawers, they are both useful and charming, and always welcome as gifts. They are a lovely way to use small amounts of the most luxurious materials. If you build up a collection of beautiful fabrics, such as fine linens, old lace and shimmering organza, to complement your own home-made potpourri, you will have all you need to make sachets that not only smell sweet but look lovely too.

POTPOURRI RECIPES AND MIXES

The name "potpourri" literally means rot-pot, and there are two distinct ways of making it. The moist method, which has the longer pedigree, results in a fragrant mixture which is best kept in perforated containers for its scent to be enjoyed. The dry method is more straightforward and gives attractive-looking results which can be displayed in open bowls. To make potpourri by the dry

method you can dry plant materials over an extended period, spanning several seasons; don't forget to save off-cuts from dried-flower arrangements for use in your potpourri mixes.

MAKING POTPOURRI

The dry method of making potpourri is the most convenient, but you might like to try the more traditional moist method which was used in Elizabethan times.

MOIST METHOD

This old method of making potpourri consists of layering partially dried flowers, petals and leaves with salt in a moisture-proof lidded box (this must not be made of metal). The salt acts as a desiccant and draws out the natural moisture in the plant materials. The box is covered and set aside for 10 days, after which the mixture will have fermented and formed a solid block. This is broken up, placed in a jar or crock and blended with powdered spices and a fixative, as for the dry method. It is then set aside, except for daily stirring, for 6 weeks. A few drops of an essential plant oil, such as attar of roses, may then be added to the mixture. After a further 2 weeks the potpourri will be ready for use.

ELIZABETHAN MOIST POTPOURRI

Use this old-fashioned recipe to capture the evocative fragrance of a midsummer garden when the roses are in full flower.

- about 1 kg (2¼ lb) fresh scented rose petals
- 200 g (7 oz/¾ cup) sea salt
- lidded container
- mixing bowl
- 45 ml (3 tbsp) ground allspice
- 30 ml (2 tbsp) ground cloves
- 45 ml (3 tbsp) brown sugar
- 60 ml (4 tbsp) ground orris root
- 15 ml (1 tbsp) brandy
- 15 g (½ oz) fresh lavender flowers
- 15 g (½ oz) fresh lemon verbena leaves
- 15 g (½ oz) fresh scented pelargonium leaves

Mix the rose petals and the salt together. Seal the container and leave for about 3–4 days. Transfer the petals into a large bowl and add the remaining ingredients, one by one, stirring well. Cover the mixture and stir every couple of days for 2 weeks. After about 3 weeks decant the moist mixture into jars with perforated lids.

DRY METHOD

This kind of potpourri is a decorative blend of pre-dried flowers, petals and leaves with spices and a few drops of essential oil to enhance the aroma. Add ground spices such as cinnamon, allspice, cloves, mace or nutmeg. The mixture also needs a fixative, such as ground orris root or gum benzoin (benjamin), to stop the fragrance evaporating.

As a general guide, to every litre (1¾ pints/4 cups) of dried plant material allow 30–45 ml (2–3 tbsp) powdered spices, 30 ml (2 tbsp) ground orris root or other fixative, a strip of dried citrus peel and 2 drops of an essential oil. Place the dried plant materials, spices and fixative in a lidded ceramic or glass container and stir them daily with a spoon or with your fingers – this is a very therapeutic part of the process – for up to 6 weeks. Add the oil and set aside, stirring with a spoon every day or so, for another 2 weeks.

If your potpourri loses some of the intensity of its aroma over time, revive it by stirring in another 2–3 drops of essential oil or, if you've run out, a few drops of brandy. To help retain the colours of the petals, keep the potpourri away from bright sunlight.

SPICY ORANGE POTPOURRI

The basis of this simple mixture is dried orange rind, a perfect background to the warm spicy scent of the other ingredients.

- 25 g (1 oz) coriander seeds
- 25 g (1 oz) whole cloves
- 50 g (2 oz) star anise
- 15 g (½ oz) cinnamon bark, crumbled
- 15 g (½ oz) allspice berries
- dried rind of 2 oranges, crumbled
- 15 ml (1 tbsp) ground cinnamon
- 15 ml (1 tbsp) ground orris root
- mixing bowl
- mixing spoon
- lidded container

Mix all the ingredients together and set them aside in a lidded container for 6 weeks, stirring daily to blend the aromas.

ROSE PETAL AND LAVENDER POTPOURRI

Pick rose petals from full-blown roses for this summer mixture.

- 475 ml (16 fl oz/2 cups) dried rose petals
- 250 ml (8 fl oz/1 cup) dried lavender flowers
- 250 ml (8 fl oz/1 cup) dried herb leaves, such as pineapple mint, thyme or lemon verbena
- 15 ml (1 tbsp) ground cinnamon
- 15 ml (1 tbsp) ground allspice
- 30 ml (2 tbsp) ground orris root
- 2 drops lavender oil
- mixing bowl
- mixing spoon
- lidded container

Mix ingredients as for Spicy Orange Potpourri.

POTPOURRI MIXES

*Most of the following mixes are made using the dry method, which is suitable for any of the projects in the book,
or you can simply place them in an attractive bowl to scent your home.*

HERBAL POTPOURRI

A quick mixture that will scent the room delightfully.

- 1 handful dried mint leaves
- 2 handfuls dried marigold flowers
- 1 handful any other dried herbs, such as thyme, sage or marjoram
- 10 slices dried orange
- 6 cinnamon sticks
- a few dried chillies
- 4 nutmegs
- 5 ml (1 tsp) mint essential oil
- 15 ml (1 tbsp) sweet orange essential oil
- mixing bowl
- large plastic bag
- 15 ml (1 tbsp) ground orris root

1 Mix all the ingredients, except for the orris root, together in the bowl. Make sure the oils are well mixed with all the other ingredients.

2 Tip the mixture into a large plastic bag, add the orris root and shake well. Leave to mature for 1–2 weeks, shaking occasionally. Then display the mixture in a suitable bowl or dish.

COTTAGE-GARDEN MIX

Make this pretty, delicately scented mixture in the same way as Herbal Potpourri.

- 250 ml (8 fl oz/1 cup) dried lavender flowers
- 250 ml (8 fl oz/1 cup) dried rose petals
- 250 ml (8 fl oz/1 cup) dried dianthus flowers
- 250 ml (8 fl oz/1 cup) dried scented pelargonium leaves
- 15 ml (1 tbsp) ground cinnamon
- 10 ml (2 tsp) ground allspice
- 5 ml (1 tsp) dried grated lemon rind
- 3 drops rose essential oil
- 3 drops geranium essential oil
- mixing bowl
- mixing spoon
- large plastic bag
- 30 ml (2 tbsp) ground orris root

WOODLAND MIX

Follow the steps for Herbal Potpourri to make this unusual spicy potpourri recipe.

- 250 ml (8 fl oz/1 cup) lime seedpods or "keys"
- 250 ml (8 fl oz/1 cup) cedar bark shavings
- 250 ml (8 fl oz/1 cup) sandalwood shavings
- 250 ml (8 fl oz/1 cup) cones
- 15 ml (1 tbsp) whole cloves
- 15 ml (1 tbsp) star anise
- 1 cinnamon stick, crushed
- 4 drops sandalwood essential oil
- 2 drops cinnamon essential oil
- mixing bowl
- mixing spoon
- large plastic bag
- 30 ml (2 tbsp) ground orris root

ROSE AND DELPHINIUM POTPOURRI

*The addition of mint leaves lends a cool note to this
summer garden mixture.*

- 250 g (9 oz) dried scented rose
  petals
- 90 g (3 ½ oz) dried delphinium
  flowers and marigold petals
- mixing bowl
- 15 ml (1 tbsp) dried mint leaves
- 5 ml (1 tsp) ground cloves

- 5 ml (1 tsp) ground cinnamon
- 5 ml (1 tsp) ground allspice
- 15 ml (1 tbsp) ground orris root
- 8 drops rose essential oil
- mixing spoon
- lidded container

Mix the petals and flowers together in a large bowl, then add each of
the other ingredients, stirring well after each addition. Put the mixture
into a lidded container and leave for 6 weeks.

CITRUS AND ROSE-SCENTED POTPOURRI

*Lemon balm and dried lemon rind are a refreshing complement to the
sweetly scented rose petals in this potpourri.*

- 250 g (9 oz) dried scented rose
  petals
- 90 g (3½ oz) dried lavender and
  lemon balm
- lidded container
- dried grated rind of 2 large
  lemons

- 5 ml (1 tsp) ground allspice
- 5 ml (1 tsp) ground orris
  root
- mixing spoon

Mix the flowers and herbs together in an airtight container, add the
lemon rind and leave for 2–3 days. Add the spices and orris root,
stir well and leave for 6 weeks, stirring occasionally.

ORCHID BLEND

This is a romantic and pretty way to preserve the memory of a special gift of orchids or other luxurious flowers.

- 250 ml (8 fl oz/1 cup) dried orchid flowers
- 250 ml (8 fl oz/1 cup) dried carnation petals
- 250 ml (8 fl oz/1 cup) dried peony petals
- 250 ml (8 fl oz/1 cup) dried marjoram leaves

- 15 ml (1 tbsp) ground ginger
- 5 ml (1 tsp) ground cloves
- 30 ml (2 tbsp) ground orris root
- 2 drops carnation essential oil
- lidded container
- mixing spoon

Mix all the ingredients together and set them aside in a lidded container for 4 weeks, stirring daily to blend the aromas.

MARIGOLD MIXTURE

This summer blend of garden flowers and petals is made by the moist method. Use it to fill a perforated potpourri jar.

- 475 ml (16 fl oz/2 cups) partially dried rose petals
- 250 ml (8 fl oz/1 cup) partially dried marigold petals
- 250 ml (8 fl oz/1 cup) partially dried delphinium flowers
- 50 g (2 oz) salt

- airtight container
- 15 ml (1 tbsp) ground coriander
- 5 ml (1 tsp) grated nutmeg
- 5 ml (1 tsp) ground cloves
- 30 ml (2 tbsp) ground orris root
- 2 drops oil of cloves

Mix the petals, flowers and salt and leave in an airtight container for 10 days. When the mixture has formed a solid block, break it up and mix in the spices and ground orris root. Leave for 6 weeks, then add a few drops of the essential oil. Leave for another 2 weeks before using.

SUMMER POTPOURRI

Gather a few flowers each time you go out, and place them on a wire rack in a warm place to dry. Pick rose petals from full-blown roses, spread them out to dry and use them as the base for the potpourri.

- 15 ml (1 tbsp) ground cinnamon
- 15 ml (1 tbsp) ground orris root
- 1 whole nutmeg, grated
- pestle and mortar
- 40 drops lavender essential oil
- 40 drops rose geranium essential oil
- 10 drops mandarin essential oil
- 1.75 litres (3 pints/ 7½ cups) dried flower petals and heads (rose petals, rosebuds, peonies, lavender, pink peppercorns)
- mixing bowl
- lidded container

Mix together the cinnamon, orris root and nutmeg in a mortar. Add the essential oils and blend to a moist powder using a pestle. Measure the flower petals and heads into a large mixing bowl and blend thoroughly with the oil and spice mixture. Place the potpourri in a lidded container and leave for 6 weeks, stirring occasionally.

AUTUMN POTPOURRI

The subtle, mellow colours of autumn are beautifully captured in this attractive potpourri with its orange and green physalis (Chinese lanterns) mixed with oak leaves, acorns and cones. An unusual blend of spices and oils gives the mixture a clean, tangy fragrance.

- 15 ml (1 tbsp) freshly ground coarse black pepper
- 15 ml (1 tbsp) freshly ground coriander
- 5 ml (1 tsp) ground ginger
- 30 ml (2 tbsp) gum benzoin (benjamin)
- mortar and pestle
- 20 drops ginger essential oil
- 20 drops lime essential oil
- 5 drops basil essential oil
- 5 drops juniper essential oil
- 1.75 litres (3 pints/7½ cups) leaves and seeds (orange and green physalis, oak leaves, acorns, seed-heads, small cones and golden mushrooms)
- mixing bowl
- lidded container

Mix the spices and the gum benzoin (benjamin) together in a mortar. Use a pestle to blend in the oils to make a moist powder. Measure the leaves and seeds into a large bowl and add the oil and spice mixture. Place the potpourri in a lidded container and leave for 6 weeks, shaking occasionally.

SPICE ISLANDS POTPOURRI

An exotic blend of nuts, pods, spices and chillies with spice and wood oils.

- 10 ml (2 tsp) ground star anise
- 5 ml (1 tsp) ground nutmeg
- 5 ml (1 tsp) ground cinnamon
- 5 ml (1 tsp) ground allspice
- 5 ml (1 tsp) ground cloves
- 10 ml (2 tsp) gum benzoin (benjamin)
- pestle and mortar
- 25 drops cinnamon essential oil
- 10 drops ginger essential oil
- 10 drops orange essential oil
- 10 drops patchouli essential oil
- 5 drops sandalwood or vetiver essential oil
- 1.75 litres (3 pints/7½ cups) nuts and seeds (whole star anise, brazil nuts, chillies, cinnamon sticks, whole nutmegs and bakuli pods)
- mixing bowl
- lidded container

Mix the spices, gum benzoin (benjamin) and oils as for Autumn Potpourri. Mix with the nuts and seeds in a large bowl. Place the potpourri in a lidded container and leave for 6 weeks, shaking occasionally.

WINTER POTPOURRI

This potpourri is made up of materials in substantial forms – whole oranges, pomegranates, sunflower heads and rose heads with big pieces of cinnamon – because they are included for the way they look, not how they smell. Find a large, striking bowl suitable for such a magnificent mix, and use a ready-made spicy potpourri oil to scent the mixture. A final dusting with gold glitter powder gives it a festive look.

- 1 handful cloves
- 1 handful dried hibiscus buds
- 1 handful dried tulip petals
- 1 handful small cones
- 7 dried oranges
- 5 dried sunflower heads
- 1 handful dried red rose heads
- 5 small dried pomegranates
- 10 dried grapefruit slices
- glass bowl
- 10 cinnamon sticks
- spicy potpourri oil
- gold powder
- mixing spoon

1 Place all the dried ingredients except the cinnamon in a glass bowl and mix together thoroughly. Break the cinnamon sticks into large pieces and add to the mixture.

2 Add several drops of potpourri oil to the mixture. Scatter a spoonful of gold powder over and stir well to distribute the gold powder and scent throughout the potpourri.

SIMMERING POTPOURRI

Creating a pleasantly aromatic environment can have beneficial effects at home and in the office, and a simmering potpourri is very effective.

NIGHT-TIME BLEND
- 120 ml (4 fl oz/ ½ cup) dried lime flowers
- 50 ml (2 fl oz/ ¼ cup) dried chamomile flowers
- 15 ml (1 tbsp) dried sweet marjoram
- 15 ml (1 tbsp) dried lavender flowers
- heat-proof bowl
- night-light (tea-light)

REFRESHING UPLIFTING BLEND
- 120 ml (4 fl oz/ ½ cup) dried lemon verbena leaves
- 50 ml (2 fl oz/ ¼ cup) dried jasmine flowers
- 30 ml (2 tbsp) dried lemon rind
- 5 ml (1 tsp) coriander seeds
- heat-proof bowl
- night-light (tea-light)

Place a mixture of scented flowers and leaves (without any fixatives or additives) in a bowl of water and heat gently from below – a candle or night-light (tea-light) may be sufficient. Compared with dry potpourri, the simmering variety does not last for long, but it smells much stronger for a while. Try making your own blends, using your nose to achieve the aroma you desire. Add about 250 ml (8 fl oz/1 cup) dried material to 1.2 litres (2 pints/5 cups) water.

Do not leave the candle or night-light (tea-light) burning unattended.

SWEET-SCENTED SACHETS

*L*ittle bags and decorative sachets filled with mixtures of flowers, herbs and spices can be used to disperse subtle fragrances all around your home. They couldn't be easier to make, and  are an ideal way to make use of your fabric scraps. Tuck them into drawers or hang them in the wardrobe, where they will not only keep

 your clothes smelling fresh and sweet but will also keep clothes moths at bay. Fill a muslin bag with fresh herbs to perfume your bath-water and leave a pretty petal-filled bag hanging in a guest room.

SOOTHING BATH SACHET

Pamper a busy friend with the ingredients for a traditional herbal bath by filling a fine muslin bag with relaxing herbs.
The bag can be tied to the taps so that the hot water runs through it. This drawstring design means that the bag can be re-used
time after time if it is filled with fresh herbs. Chamomile and hops are relaxing; basil and sage are invigorating.

- silky muslin,
  30 x 40 cm
  (12 x 16 in)
- pins
- matching sewing
  thread
- needle

- scissors
- cotton fabric
  scraps, for casing
- 1 m (1 yd) narrow
  ribbon
- safety pin
- dried herbs to fill

1 With right sides together, fold over about 5 cm (2 in) of the silky muslin at both short ends. Pin and stitch each short side seam leaving a 1 cm (½ in) seam allowance. Trim the seams and turn the ends right-side out.

2 Press flat then turn in the raw edges of the folded ends, pin and sew a narrow hem.

3 Cut two strips of cotton, 3 cm (1¼ in) wide, to fit across the width of the muslin plus 1 cm (½ in). Turn in and press 5 mm (¼ in) hems all round each strip. Hem the ends, then pin to the right side of the muslin so that the lower edges of the casings line up with the hems. Neatly stitch along both long edges.

4 With right sides together, fold the muslin in half so the casings line up. Stitch the side seams from the bottom edge of the casing to the bottom edge of the bag. Trim the seams.

5 Cut the ribbon in half, attach a safety pin to one end of one piece and thread it through both casings so that both ends finish up at the same side. Repeat with the other piece, threading it in the other direction. Fill the bag with herbs ready for use.

EMBROIDERED LACY SACHET

A beautiful trimming of white Austrian lace adds the finishing touch to this charming little cross-stitch design.
Use your favourite mix of potpourri to fill the sachet.

- white 14 hpi aida, two 13 x 15 cm (5 x 6 in) pieces
- stranded embroidery thread (floss) in red and mid-blue
- tapestry needle
- 1 m (1 yd) of Austrian lace, 4 cm (1½ in) wide
- tacking (basting) thread
- sewing needle
- pins
- 15 cm (6 in) narrow red ribbon
- sewing machine
- white sewing thread
- scissors
- potpourri sachet
- polyester wadding (batting), two 10 x 13 cm (4 x 5 in) pieces

1 Find the centre of one piece of aida and, following the chart, work the cross-stitch using two strands of embroidery thread (floss) and the backstitch using one strand. Press the embroidery on the reverse side.

2 To make up the sachet, gather the lace and pin round the edge of the embroidered panel. Adjust the gathers and tack (baste). Fold the ribbon in half and pin to a top corner with the loop facing inward.

3 With the embroidery and lace to the inside, stitch round three sides. Trim the seams and corners and turn through. Put the potpourri sachet between the layers of wadding (batting) and insert into the cover. Slip stitch the opening to finish.

ROSE-SCENTED SACHETS

*A gossamer fabric bag filled with scented rose heads and petals is a
delightfully feminine accessory for a guest room.
Keep the flowers lightly perfumed by adding a few drops of
rose essential oil or potpourri refresher. Choose either extremely
fine fabric or an open-weave linen or muslin that will allow the
perfume to seep through it.*

- outer fabric (organza, linen or
  muslin), 36 x 23 cm
  (14 x 9 in)
- matching or contrasting lining
  fabric, 36 x 23 cm (14 x 9 in)
- pins
- sewing machine

- matching sewing thread
- scissors
- 1 m (1 yd)
  co-ordinating cord
- safety pin
- 2 matching tassels
- dried scented rose petals

1 Stitch the two pieces of fabric
right sides together around all four
edges, leaving a 4 cm (1½ in) gap
in one side. Turn through, press
and slip stitch the opening. About
one-quarter of the way down, run
two lines of stitching across the
width of the bag, 2 cm (¾ in)
apart, to accommodate the
drawstring. Fold the bag in half
with right sides together and sew
up the bottom and side seams.
Turn right sides out and press.

2 Make a small snip in the outer
fabric of the drawstring casing at
the side seam to allow the
drawstring through. Take care not
to cut through the lining. Double
the cord and whipstitch the ends
together. Use a safety pin to feed
it all the way round the bag and
out at the other side of the seam
through a second small hole.
Adjust the cord so that the join is
inside the casing. Thread a tassel
on to each cord loop and secure.

3 Fill the bag with scented rose
petals. Pull the cord tight to create
gathers in the neck of the bag and
tie the ends in a knot.

Decorated Sachets

Several of these aromatic sachets kept among the linen in the airing cupboard will impart a fragrance that makes clean sheets even more inviting. Lavender is also a very effective clothes-moth deterrent.

- small calico or muslin bags
- lavender flowers
- elastic bands
- ribbon
- selection of dried flowers and herbs
- glue gun

1 Fill each bag with the dried lavender flowers, and secure with an elastic band. Do not overfill the bags or the necks will be difficult to secure.

2 Tie the neck of each bag with a ribbon and decorate with a selection of dried flowers and herbs, attached with a glue gun.

HERBAL MOTH BAG MIXTURE

Moths dislike any pungent herbal fragrance. In addition to lavender, herbs such as tansy and southernwood work very effectively, and you could also add thyme, mugwort, woodruff or sweet marjoram. The cinnamon and orris root will ensure that the moth bags remain effective for a longer period.

- 475 ml (16 fl oz/ 2 cups) dried lavender flowers
- 250 ml (8 fl oz/1 cup) dried tansy leaves
- 475 ml (16 fl oz/ 2 cups) dried southernwood
- 2 crushed cinnamon sticks
- 5 ml (1 tsp) ground orris root

ROSE SACHET MIXTURE

Fill little bags with this fragrant mixture to keep your clothes smelling delicious.

- 75 g (3 oz) scented red rose petals
- 5 ml (1 tsp) ground orris root
- 25 drops rose essential oil

FOLK-ART LAVENDER SACHETS

Use fabric scraps to appliqué simple motifs on to charming checked fabrics, and then stitch them into sachets to fill with lavender and use as drawer-fresheners. Inspired by traditional folk art, these will appeal to everyone.

- scissors
- fabric scraps
- paper for templates
- pencil
- pins
- sewing needle
- tacking (basting) thread

- matching sewing thread
- stranded embroidery thread (floss) in contrasting colours
- button
- loose dried lavender

1 Cut two squares of fabric to a size of about 15 cm (6 in). If you are using a checked fabric, let the design dictate the exact size. Scale up the template and use it as a pattern to cut bird and wing shapes from contrasting fabrics.

2 Pin and tack (baste) the bird shape in the centre of the right side of the sachet front. Neatly slip stitch the bird shape to the sachet front, turning in the edges as you go. Repeat with the wing shape.

3 Using three strands of embroidery thread (floss) in a contrasting colour, make neat running stitches around the bird and its wing. Make long stitches on the tail and wing to indicate feathers. Sew on the button eye.

4 With right sides facing, stitch the front and back of the sachet together, leaving a 5 cm (2 in) gap. Trim the seams. Turn the sachet right side out and press. Fill with dried lavender, then slip stitch to close the gap.

ORGANZA LAVENDER CUSHION

Dried lavender flowers, seen through translucent organza, contribute to the design of this exquisite cushion with their soft indigo colour and unique texture, while releasing a wonderful fragrance to scent the whole room. The backing is made of linen, to add weight and substance to the cushion.

- purple linen 30 cm (12 in) square
- purple metal-shot organza 30 cm (12 in) square
- pins
- tacking (basting) thread
- needle
- sewing machine
- sewing thread
- dried lavender
- scissors
- 1.5 m (1½ yd) wide ribbon
- 1.5 m (1½ yd) narrow ribbon
- 4 gold tassels

1 With wrong sides together, lay the organza over the linen and hem all round both squares. Pin and tack (baste). Stitch, leaving a 10 cm (4 in) gap. Measure the combined widths of the ribbons and mark this amount in from each side of the cushion. Stitch this inner square, leaving a corresponding gap.

2 Fill the middle section of the cushion with lavender. Stitch across the gap in the inner seam to enclose the lavender, then stitch across the gap in the outer stitching to neaten.

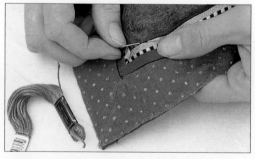

3 Cut 4 lengths of the wide ribbon 1 cm (½ in) longer than the width of the cushion. Make a diagonal fold in each end of the ribbon at each corner and trim the ends to leave a 5 mm (¼ in) seam allowance.

4 Join the lengths of ribbon along the fold lines. Slip stitch the outside edge of the ribbon to the outside edge of the cushion, then repeat with the inside edge.

5 Repeat the last two steps with the narrow ribbon, placing it between the wide ribbon and the inner stitching line. Hand sew a tassel to each corner at the back of the cushion.

SHAKER-STYLE SACHET

These delightful country-style sachets are Shaker-inspired, being made in natural cotton checked fabrics and decorated with simple sprigs of fresh lavender. The heart was a favourite Shaker motif, symbolic of their saying, "Hands to work and heart to God". The sachets are attached to wires and could be hung inside a cabinet to scent its contents.

- paper for template
- pencil
- scissors
- checked cotton fabric 50 x 25 cm (20 x 10 in)
- pins
- sewing needle

- matching sewing thread
- loose dried lavender
- wire
- 6 sprigs dried lavender
- raffia or ribbon

1 Draw a heart-shaped template about 20 cm (8 in) high and use it to cut out two fabric hearts. With right sides facing, stitch them together around the outside edges, leaving a 5 cm (2 in) gap along one straight side. Trim the seams and clip around the curves.

2 Turn the heart right side out through the gap and fill generously with loose, dried lavender. Slip stitch to close the gap. Bend both ends of a 30 cm (12 in) length of wire into hooks and hook them into the seam at the top of the heart. Bend the hooks closed.

3 Make two bunches of three sprigs of lavender, using wire to secure, then cross these over each other and wire together. Tie them with raffia or ribbon and stitch to the front of the heart.

Scented lace cushion and sachets

Making this cushion could not be simpler – it requires no sewing at all, just a safety pin! The lace is fine enough to allow the rose-petal scent to permeate a clothes drawer or a pile of pillows on a bed. From time to time a little essential oil or potpourri refreshing perfume will be needed to refresh the scent.

- 2 pieces of fine lace fabric, 25 cm (10 in) square
- sharp-pointed scissors
- 1 m (1 yd) each of thin silk ribbon in two colours
- safety pin
- rose-scented potpourri

Tiny sachets can also be made very quickly from circles of the thinnest muslin or by using lace handkerchiefs. Make a small pile of potpourri in the centre of the circle, gather the fabric together and tie securely with a fine ribbon.

1 Place the fabric pieces together, then with the scissors make small cuts through both layers of fabric 2 cm (¾ in) from the edge and at small intervals all the way round.

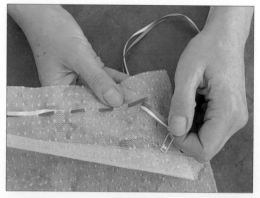

2 Attaching one end of both pieces of ribbon to the safety pin, thread it through the holes, leaving a small gap on one side of the cushion for filling with the potpourri.

3 Fill the cushion with the rose-scented potpourri through the opening. Crush or tear the larger petals or rose heads to fit through the small gap.

4 When the cushion is filled, continue threading the ribbon, cut it to length and tie in a bow. If you pull the ribbon tight, you can give the hem a ruched effect.

FRAGRANT
HOME ACCESSORIES

The delicate natural scents of potpourri and herbs can be used to enhance your home in many ways, even if they no longer play such an essential part in keeping it sweet-smelling as they did in the Middle Ages. Garlands of herbs and whole spices are a perfect decoration for a kitchen wall, and are also a practical way

to keep ingredients to hand. Fill pretty cushions with floral mixtures for a delicious waft of scent as you sink into a chair, or with relaxing hops and chamomile to help you sleep.

BAY AND APPLE KITCHEN HANGING

*The dried apple slices in this garland are echoed in the cross-stitch apple
motif on the little cushion; filled with potpourri,
this hanging will add a subtle fragrance to your kitchen.*

- 28 hpi cream evenweave linen,
  15 x 30 cm (6 x 12 in)
- scissors
- tacking (basting) thread
- interlocking bar frame
- stranded embroidery thread
  (floss) as listed in key
- tapestry needle
- sewing machine
- matching sewing thread
- potpourri
- 5 cm (2 in) ribbon or tape,
  15 mm (⅝ in) wide
- pins
- 45 cm (18 in) garden wire
- bay leaves
- dried apple slices

1 Cut the linen into two squares
measuring 15 cm (6 ins). Tack
(baste) guidelines across the middle
of one piece in both directions,
insert in frame and work the
cross-stitch following the chart at
the back of the book, using two
strands of embroidery thread
(floss) over two threads. Work the
backstitch using one strand, then
press on the reverse side.

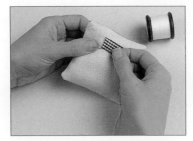

2 Join the two squares of linen,
right sides together. Stitch two
threads away from the cross-stitch
and leave a 5 cm (2 in) opening at
the bottom. Trim the seams and
corners and turn through. Fill
with potpourri and slip stitch the
gap. Fold in the ends of the
ribbon and pin to the back of the
cushion, 2 cm (¾ in) from the top.
Oversew along both long sides.

3 Bend the garden wire into a
circle. Thread the cushion on to
the wire. Make small holes in the
bay leaves and apple slices and
thread alternately on to the wire.
Some of the larger bay leaves are
bent over and threaded on again
to create a looser effect. Oversew
the corners of the cushion to
secure it on the wire. Hook the
ends of the wire together.

ROSE AND POTPOURRI GARLAND

This delicate and pretty garland can be hung on a wall or door, or you could use it as
an effective table decoration. It uses a hop vine ring as its base; try to keep the flowers and other decorations
light and simple in keeping with its informal rustic style.

- dried roses
- scissors
- all-purpose glue or glue gun
- hop vine or twig ring
- moss
- potpourri
- fir cones
- raffia

1 Cut off the stems of the roses and glue the heads to the ring, some in pairs and others as single roses. Try to achieve a good balance. Next, glue hanks of moss to the ring in the gaps between the roses. Apply generous quantities of glue directly on to the ring and sprinkle on handfuls of potpourri, to cover the glue completely.

2 Finally, add the fir cones, gluing them on to the ring singly or in pairs. Finish the project by tying a raffia bow, if you wish.

HERBS ON A ROPE

Fill these five pretty gingham bags, each embellished with a cross-stitch heart, with herbal potpourri and hang them on the kitchen wall.

- white 16 hpi aida, 10 x 15 cm (4 x 6 in)
- scissors
- stranded embroidery thread (floss) in red and dark blue
- embroidery needle
- dark blue denim, 25 x 15 cm (10 x 6 in)
- pins
- pinking shears
- five red and blue check cotton fabrics, 15 x 20 cm (6 x 8 in) each
- all-purpose glue
- sewing machine
- matching sewing thread
- dried herb mixture
- 2.5 cm (1 in) brass curtain ring
- 1 m (1 yd) heavyweight cotton cord
- coarse string

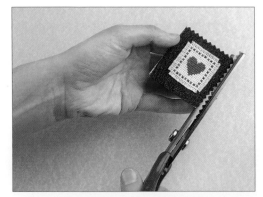

1 Cut five 4.5 cm (1¾ in) squares out of the aida. Following the chart, work a red cross-stitch heart in the middle of each piece using three strands of embroidery thread (floss), then complete the red cross-stitch border.
Cut five 7 cm (2¾ in) denim squares and pin the embroidered pieces to them. Work the blue cross-stitch through both layers. Fray the edges of the aida squares and trim the edges of the denim with pinking shears.

2 Glue each heart motif to the centre of a check rectangle, 4 cm (1½ in) from the lower long edge. Fold in half, wrong sides together, and stitch the short edges together. Position this seam at the centre back and stitch along the bottom edge. Trim the corners and turn through.

3 Trim the top edge with pinking shears and work a row of running stitches 4 cm (1½ in) from the top. Fill the bags with herbs, pull up the running stitches and fasten securely.

4 Thread the brass ring on to the cord, fold it in half and bind the top with string to secure. Tie the bags on to the doubled cord at intervals using short lengths of string.

HERB POT-STAND

Sew an aromatic sachet, filled with cinnamon, cloves and bay leaves, to protect tabletops from hot pots and pans.
The heat immediately releases the piquant aroma of the filling. The sachet is made from cotton ticking, perfectly set off by
the mattress-style ties which keep the contents evenly distributed.

- cotton ticking,
  62 x 55 cm
  (25 x 22 in)
- scissors
- matching sewing
  thread
- needle
- iron

- pins
- dried bay leaves,
  cloves and small
  cinnamon sticks
- heavy-duty
  upholstery needle
- fine cotton string

1 To make the hanger, cut a strip of ticking
5 x 30 cm (2 x 12 in). With right sides facing,
fold this in half lengthways. Stitch the long
side, leaving the ends open. Trim the seam.
Turn right side out and press. Fold in half to
form a loop. Cut two rectangles of fabric
measuring 31 x 50 cm (12½ x 20 in).

2 Place the two pieces right sides together,
then slip the hanging loop between the layers,
with the raw edges pointing out towards one
corner. Pin and stitch the pieces together,
leaving a 7.5 cm (3 in) gap open in one side.
Trim the seams. Turn the mat right side out.

3 Fill the cushion loosely with the herbs and
spices. Slip stitch the opening securely.

4 Thread the heavy-duty upholstery needle
with cotton string, stitch through both layers
about one-third of the way in from two sides of
the mat. Clear the filling away from the area
as you go. Knot the string and fray the ends.
Make three more ties in the same way.

FRAGRANT HERB PILLOW

This lovely scented sachet looks as if it has been thickly encrusted with gold. It's made using a cutwork technique in which the different fabrics are revealed as if by magic. It's enjoyable to make and a wonderful gift to receive. Choose fabrics of similar weights but contrasting textures and shades of gold, such as taffeta, organza and lamé.

- four 17 cm (6½ in) squares of different gold fabrics
- pins
- matching sewing thread
- sewing machine
- sharp-pointed scissors
- two 25 cm (10 in) squares of gold fabric chosen from the selection above
- gold braid
- needle
- fragrant herbs or potpourri

1 Pin the four 17 cm (6½ in) squares of different gold fabrics together, all with right sides facing up.

2 Sewing through all four layers, machine stitch across the middle of the square in both directions, then stitch a simple star motif in each quarter. Don't worry if the stars don't match each other exactly: you are aiming for a freehand effect.

3 With the point of the scissors, pierce the top layer of fabric and cut out a section of a star. Work around each star, cutting through different areas and layers to reveal the one below until you are pleased with the effect.

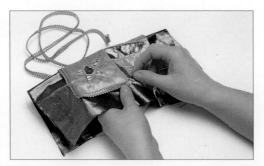

4 Pin the appliqué square in the centre of the right side of one of the large squares and machine stitch all around the edge. Hand-stitch a length of gold braid over the seam to hide the raw edges.

5 Pin the other gold square to the front of the cushion, right sides together, and stitch around the edge with a 1 cm (½ in) seam allowance, leaving an opening down one side. Turn through, fill loosely with the scented herbs or potpourri and slip stitch the opening.

Herb-filled Sleep Pillow

Many people still swear by traditional sleep pillows filled with chamomile, which helps you to relax, and hops, which induce a feeling of sleepy well-being. Stitch a pillow filled with these relaxing herbs and make a gift of a good night's sleep.

- linen muslin, 2 m x 20 cm (2 yd x 8 in) – this can be made up of two or more shorter lengths
- sewing needle
- matching sewing thread
- scissors
- cotton fabric, 50 x 25 cm (20 x 10 in)
- pins
- herbal sleep mix
- 1 m (1 yd) antique lace
- 1 m (1 yd) ribbon, 1 cm (½ in) wide
- 4 pearl buttons

*Y*ou can buy a ready-prepared herbal sleep mix, or make up your own using dried chamomile, lemon verbena and a few hops.

1 Join the linen muslin lengths to make up a strip 2 m (2 yd) long. With right sides facing, stitch the ends of the strip together to form a ring. Trim the seam. Fold the muslin in half lengthways with wrong sides facing and run a line of gathering stitches close to the raw edges. Cut the cotton fabric into two 25 cm (10 in) squares.

2 Pull up the gathering threads of the muslin to fit the cushion edge. Pin it to the right side of one square, with the raw edges matching, easing the gathers evenly round the cushion. Put the second square on top, right sides together, and pin the corners. Stitch the seams, leaving a 5 cm (2 in) gap for inserting the filling. Trim the seams.

3 Turn the cushion right side out and fill it with herbal sleep mix. Stitch the gap to enclose the border. Using tiny stitches, sew the lace to the cushion about 2.5 cm (1 in) away from the border.

4 Stitch the ribbon close to the lace, making a neat diagonal fold at the corners, and finish by sewing a tiny pearl button to each corner.

PERFUMED
DECORATIVE GIFTS

otpourri mixtures and scented sachets  both make ideal gifts at any time of the year. They are especially suitable for Christmas, when you can suit the season with warm spicy aromas, or make generous offerings of flowers and herbs harvested from your own garden and dried during the autumn.

No one can have too many beautiful scented bags or sachets – there  is always another drawer into which one can be tucked. Be lavish with the quality of the materials you use: you need only a few scraps so for very little cost you can make some really luxurious gifts.

SCENTED VELVET CUSHIONS

The cotton velvet for these cushions was hand-dyed to obtain the soft, rich shades. This is a simple process,
but store-bought colours are just as suitable. The cushions are filled with potpourri and appliquéd with nostalgic designs of
clasped hands, hearts, and doves carrying love letters.

To make the square cushion:
- scissors
- main colour velvet, 36 x 90 cm (14 x 36 in)
- contrasting velvet, 13 x 23 cm (5 x 9 in)
- metallic organza, 13 x 23 cm (5 x 9 in)
- pins
- needle
- tacking (basting) thread
- tissue paper
- pencil
- embroidery hoop (frame)
- sewing machine
- matching sewing thread
- metallic thread
- seven 20 cm (8 in) squares of polyester wadding (batting)
- potpourri
- 4 gold tassels

1 Cut two 7.5 x 23 cm (3 x 9 in) pieces of velvet for the border of the cushion front and a central panel 13 x 23 cm (5 x 9 in) in the contrasting velvet. With long sides together, join the borders to the central panel.

2 Pin and tack (baste) the organza to the right side of the central panel, squaring up the weave of the fabric. Trace your design on to a piece of tissue paper and tack to the back of the panel.

3 Stretch the piece in an embroidery hoop (frame) and work over the design using a straight stitch through both layers of fabric. Remove from the hoop (frame) and trim away the excess organza from the edges of the design.

4 Replace the piece in the hoop right side up. Thread the machine with metallic thread and sew a narrow zig-zag over the straight stitch to secure the raw edges.

5 Cut two 18 x 23 cm (7 x 9 in) pieces of main colour velvet for the back of the cushion. Turn under and stitch one long side of each piece. With right sides together, pin the back pieces to the front so that one hemmed edge overlaps the other. Sew all round the edge, leaving a 1 cm (½ in) seam allowance. Trim the seam and turn through.

6 Make the cushion pad by stacking the squares of wadding (batting) together, layering potpourri between them. Sew together through all the layers close to the edge. Place inside the cushion cover. Stitch a gold tassel to each corner of the cushion.

VALENTINE KEEPSAKES

❦

Heart-shaped gifts have a special significance, whether they are given to friends and family, or exchanged by lovers.
These little cushions, with a fragrant filling of potpourri, are made from scraps of old lace, encrusted with tiny beads and
finished with gauzy ribbons to make a truly romantic gift.

- paper for template
- pencil
- scissors
- silk fabric for backing
- small piece of lace fabric
- pins
- matching sewing thread
- needle

- polyester wadding (batting)
- potpourri
- rocaille embroidery beads
- 70 cm (28 in) lace, 2 cm (¾ in) wide
- 1 m (1 yd) gauze ribbon, 4 cm (1 ½ in) wide

1 Draw and cut out a heart shape from folded paper to make a template and use it to cut out two hearts from the backing fabric and one from the lace, allowing 1 cm (½ in) seam allowance all round. Pin the three hearts together, sandwiching the lace heart between the layers of silk. Sew together, leaving a 4 cm (1½ in) gap along one straight side for turning through.

2 Turn the heart the right way out and stuff firmly, making sure that the wadding (batting) fills out the point of the heart and including some potpourri in the centre of the filling. Slip stitch the opening.

3 Sew the beads on to the lace, using them to highlight the motifs. Gather the lace edging to fit around the heart and stitch in place.

4 Cut a 30 cm (12 in) length of gauze ribbon and sew to the top of the heart to form a hanging loop. Make a bow from the rest of the ribbon and sew to the base of the loop.

LACY POTPOURRI HEART

The ribbons and lace on this exquisitely pretty heart-shaped sachet give it an unashamedly romantic feel,
like a Victorian valentine card.

- paper for template
- pencil
- scissors
- silky muslin,
  60 x 20 cm
  (24 x 8 in)
- pins
- tacking (basting)
  thread
- matching sewing
  thread
- needle
- red stranded

- embroidery thread
  (floss)
- pearl button
- potpourri
- 50 cm (20 in)
  antique lace
- 50 cm (20 in)
  very narrow
  green satin
  ribbon
- 50 cm (20 in) green
  chiffon ribbon
  for bow

1 Make a heart-shaped paper template about 15 cm (6 in) high. Using this as a pattern, cut out four muslin hearts and tack (baste) them in two pairs so that each heart is a double thickness of muslin.

2 Cut a smaller muslin heart and attach to the front of one of the larger hearts with a row of running stitches, using two strands of embroidery thread (floss). Make another row of running stitches inside the first.

3 Use the same thread (floss) to sew on the pearl button, then make a third row of running stitches inside the other two. With right sides facing, join the two large hearts around the edges, leaving a 5 cm (2 in) gap along one of the straight sides. Trim the seams, then clip the curves and trim off the bottom point. Turn through, fill with potpourri, then slip stitch to close the gap. Slip stitch the lace around the edge.

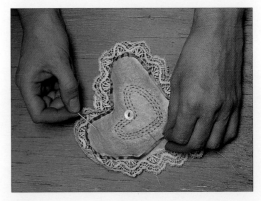

4 Stitch the narrow ribbon over the lower edge of the lace. Tie the chiffon ribbon into a bow and stitch to the heart.

EMBROIDERED POTPOURRI CUSHION

A regal little cushion embellished with a kingly lion. Before embroidering the design, back the fabric with interfacing to help it keep its shape. Pack some potpourri in amongst the filling when stuffing the cushion, to scent it.

- paper for template
- pencil
- transfer pen or dressmaker's carbon
- cream cotton, 23 cm (9 in) square
- tear-off interfacing, 23 cm (9 in) square
- tacking (basting) thread
- needle
- embroidery hoop (frame)
- stranded embroidery thread (floss) in black and

- 5 graduated shades of yellow and gold
- iron
- scissors
- dark blue velvet, 34 x 17 cm (13 x 6½ in)
- sewing machine
- matching sewing thread
- 38 cm (15 in) narrow gold cord
- polyester wadding (batting)
- potpourri
- 4 gold tassels

1 Trace the template and transfer the design on to the cotton fabric. Tack (baste) the interfacing to the back and mount in an embroidery hoop (frame). Using two strands of embroidery thread (floss), work the two circles in slip stitch in dark gold, then outline the motifs in black using straight and slip stitch.

2 Fill in the background with long and short stitches, blending the colours from light to dark gold. Remove the embroidery hoop (frame) and press the embroidery lightly on the wrong side. Cut out, leaving a 5 mm (¼ in) seam allowance. Clip the curves and tack (baste) the seam allowance to the back.

3 Cut the velvet into two 17 cm (6½ in) squares. Tack (baste) then stitch the motif to the centre front of one square. Slip stitch the gold cord around the circle. Make a small slit in the velvet and push the two ends to the wrong side. Sew over the slit to secure.

4 With right sides together, join the two squares around three sides. Clip the corners and turn. Press lightly, then fill with scented polyester wadding (batting). Slip stitch the opening and sew a tassel to each corner.

SCENTED ROSE RING

A pre-formed ring which is covered with colourful and fragrant potpourri and decorated with a pretty dried flower posy makes a romantic design for a bedroom.

- glue gun or all-purpose glue
- 20 cm (8 in) diameter stem ring
- 115 g (4 oz) potpourri
- dried flowers (such as rosebuds and sea lavender)
- florist's silver roll wire
- half a stub (floral) wire
- 1 m (1 yd) satin ribbon, 4 cm (1½ in) wide
- scissors

1 Squeeze some glue on to one area of the stem ring, allow it to cool for a few seconds, then press the potpourri on to it.

2 Work all round the ring in this way, until it is covered on all sides. Check for any gaps and fill them in. Glue some of the most colourful petals on top of the ring.

3 Arrange the dried flowers to make a small posy. Cut the stems short and bind them with florist's silver roll wire. Bend the stub (floral) wire into a U-shape, loop it over the stems and press into the ring to secure the posy on top.

4 Tie the ribbon around the stem ring, bringing the ends over the top where they will cover the posy stems and binding wire. Tie in a bow and trim the ends neatly.

Potpourri Hobby Basket

A gift basket of potpourri ingredients could be the start of a new hobby for the recipient.
Fill it with a selection of ingredients: dried flowers, spices, fixative and essential oil, together with some recipes for a variety
of aromatic blends. For a decorative touch, include a rosebud pomander, scented with cloves in the traditional way.
And to complete the floral theme, tuck in some decorated jars of rose-petal jelly.

ROSEBUD POMANDER

Until you assemble the gift basket, keep the pomander wrapped in a paper bag with some more cloves and a crumbled cinnamon stick, to retain and even intensify its aroma.

- florist's dry foam ball, 7.5 cm (3 in) diameter
- whole cloves
- 50 dried rosebuds
- scissors

- 50 cm (20 in) ribbon, 1.5 cm (⅝ in) wide
- stub (floral) wire
- wire cutters

1 Stud the foam ball all over with cloves. Cut the rose stems to about 5 cm (2 in) and press them into the foam so that the flowers just touch. Tie the ribbon into a bow. Bend half a stub (floral) wire into a U-shape, thread it through the knot in the ribbon and press it into the foam ball between the roses.

DECORATED JELLY JARS

Buy some jars of rose-petal, or any pretty-coloured jelly. Decorate with fresh rose petals on the surface of the jelly. Glue pressed petals to the outside of the jars and add a ribbon bow.

POTPOURRI IN A GAUZY BAG

Gather dried flowers or petals into a lovely pompon of metal-shot organza, tied with wide velvet ribbon in a generous bow.
It looks wonderful, smells wonderful, and prevents the potpourri from collecting dust.

- metal-shot
  organza,
  1 m (1 yd)
- scissors
- matching sewing
  thread

- needle
- 3 m (3¼ yd) narrow
  rayon ribbon
- 1 m (1 yd) wide
  velvet ribbon
- potpourri to fill

1 Cut a 40 cm (16 in) square of organza and four 40 x 10 cm (16 x 4 in) strips for the facings. With right sides together, sew a facing strip on opposite sides of the square. Sew the other strips to the two remaining sides. Trim the seams and corners and turn the facings to the wrong side.

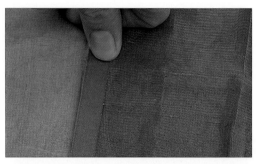

2 Top-stitch all around the edge of the square. Use the rayon ribbon to neaten the edges of the facings: cut a length of ribbon a little longer than the side of the square, turn in the ends, then stitch in place over the raw edge of the facing. Repeat on all four sides.

3 For each corner tassel, cut four lengths of rayon ribbon each about 13 cm (5 in) long, fold in half and stitch another short piece of ribbon around them near the fold. Trim the ends at an angle. Stitch a tassel to each corner.

4 Spread out the finished organza square, facing side upward. Place a handful of potpourri in the centre, then gather up all four corners to make a pouch and tie with a flamboyant velvet bow.

CHARTS AND TEMPLATES

To enlarge the templates, use either a grid system or a photocopier. For the grid system, trace the template and draw a grid of evenly spaced squares over the tracing. To scale up, draw a larger grid onto another piece of paper. Copy the outline onto the second grid by taking each square individually and drawing the relvant part of the outline in the larger square. Draw over the lines to make sure they are continuous.

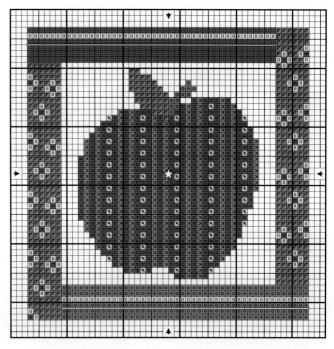

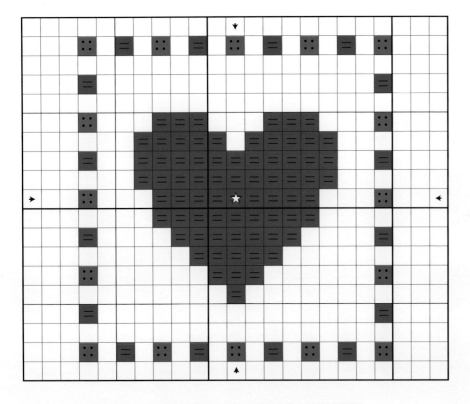

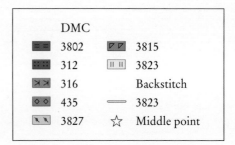

DMC

▬ ▬	3802	◱ ◱	3815
⠿ ⠿	312	‖ ‖	3823
▶ ◀	316		Backstitch
◈ ◈	435	—	3823
◺ ◺	3827	☆	Middle point

Bay and Apple Kitchen Hanging p38

DMC

▬ ▬	815
⠿ ⠿	311

☆   Middle point

Herbs on a Rope p40

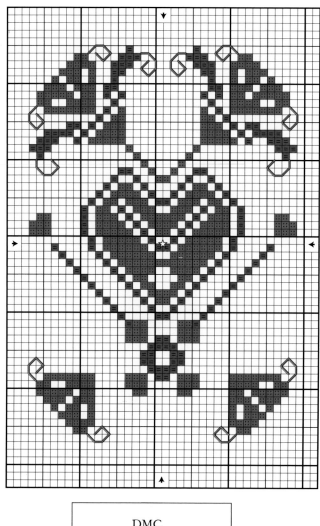

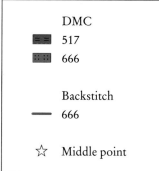

DMC

517

666

Backstitch

666

☆ Middle point

Embroidered Lacy Sachet p24

Embroidered Potpourri Cushion p56

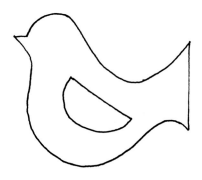

Folk-art Lavender Sachets p28

INDEX

ACKNOWLEDGEMENTS
PROJECT CONTRIBUTORS
Fiona Barnett p 18; Penny Boylan p 44; Stephanie Donaldson p 16; Mark Evans p 19; Tessa Evelegh pp 22, 28, 30, 32, 42, 46, 54, 60; Lucinda Ganderton pp 50, 52, 56; Lucie Heaton p 38; Gilly Love pp 12, 14, 25, 34; Terence Moore p 39; Katherine Richmond pp 12, 26, 27; Pamela Westland pp 11, 15, 58, 59; Dorothy Wood pp 24, 40.

PHOTOGRAPHERS
Sue Atkinson, James Duncan, Michelle Garrett, Mark Gatehouse, Nelson Hargreaves, Janine Hosegood, Don Last, Martin Norris, Debbie Patterson.